T0105889

BEST FRIENDSHIP BEACONS

B.L. Gordon

Order this book online at www.trafford.com
or email orders@trafford.com

Most Trafford titles are also available at major online book retailers.

Printed in the United States of America.

ISBN: 978-1-4669-1293-9 (sc)
ISBN: 978-1-4669-1351-6 (hc)
ISBN: 978-1-4669-1350-9 (e)

Library of Congress Control Number: 2012901902

Trafford rev. 02/23/2012

🌊 **Trafford**
PUBLISHING® www.trafford.com

North America & International
toll-free: 1 888 232 4444 (USA & Canada)
phone: 250 383 6864 ♦ fax: 812 355 4082

Best friendship Beacons

A collection of real life reflections regarding best friendship connections

Life is made more rewarding when you discover the beauty of having a lasting best friend relationship. Best friends are not restricted to certain aspects of your life. They appear in every dimension and cross all barriers, especially in regard to age, sex, race, religion, family and socio-economic barriers. They add to that feel good emotion of being alive. They help you thrive in a bevy of positive energy and you recognize that as social beings we have a plethora of resources to tap into in the quest for happiness, honesty and truth. You cannot place a value on genuine friendship and it will always stand the test of time. They can fill many shoes and wear just as many hats for you as they also journey through life with you. Most significantly, they help to give new meaning to what defines a real intangible gem of value based on a foundation of unselfish and unconditional love.

Best friends are your singing partners, your crying partners, your happy partners, and your "I can be whatever you want me to be in the moment." They willinglyhelp you in the now as you leave the past behind with the future in tow because you know that no matter what you two have discovered and although adversities sometimes stumble you, you can get back up. With a best friend who has your back then you do not need to reflect about the past or hesitate about the future as you make your next move. Life is made more beautiful when a best friend mirrors your goodness as your double. That's when you discover that you are not alone. That is the beginning of realizing that you have an inner source to your essence that reaffirms you are innately good and deserving of being happy as confirmed by the sacred spiritual union with another human being. Two individuals energetically bonding, how precious does life get?

Yours in Best Friendship,

BL Gordon

CONTENTS

1

Best Friendship and the Longevity Factor

Genuine and lasting best friendships tend to possess a longevity factor which harnesses a unique bond that surpasses interference from all types of adversities, including selfishness and aggression.

The marriage setting is a wonderful example of this type of lasting friendship. It is most notably exemplified in the fifty years and counting union of Howard and Betty Monroe. On the twenty-third of December, 2011, they celebrated their jubilee year wedding anniversary with their five children, other family members and friends. This event which was held at BankcorpSouth Conference Center in Tupelo, MS was well attended despite a cold and rainy evening. Traffic was also heavy with Christmas shoppers. Nevertheless, those in attendance at this milestone event were excited to participate in the celebration and recognition of two individuals who have demonstrated that unconditional love and long term commitment is achievable.

You were an invited guest to this happy occasion. You gladly made the hour and a half drive from Memphis despite inclimate weather and stayed overnight at the very impressive Hampton Inn & Suites/Barnes Crossing. You have always admired how the Monroes shared a happiness that for some couples becomes elusive after a few years of marriage. During this function, you observed the sparkle in their eyes whenever they looked at each other and how a smile would simultaneously appear. There was a youthfulness about them that you attributed to the genuine happiness they shared. Their laughter and joy proved to be contagious for those in attendance.

You found it interesting and most significant when Mr. Monroe shared with the attentive audience that his wife informed him when they first started dating that she was a lover not a fighter. Some of those present found this comment to be humorous, however you thought it was an important point in identifying the foundation of a relationship that has resulted in a lasting best friendship and a lasting marriage. Having known the Monroes all your life, you conclude that they do not complete each other, but instead exemplify how being true to yourself allows you to be drawn to the individual who is your equal. They also share a common spiritual background and love for family. As companions for life, the Monroe's no fighting rule demonstrates what unselfish and lasting love and friendship truly means.

Best Friends are a Merry Combination

When it comes to celebration of the Christmas holidays, three best friends appear on different parts of the spectrum. Teresa goes all out. The kid in her takes over. She is bubbly and all laughter and fun. Diane is middle of the road. She enjoys the Christmas music and the decorations. She will attend different festivities. Constance refuses to get caught up in the holiday's hustle and bustle. She wonders what all the excitement is about and never puts up any decorations. She does cook a big feast on Christmas day she states because her family expects it.

You wonder what is the common variable that draws these three middle age women together. First of all, they have been best friends since grammar school. Teresa married when she was nineteen years old. Diane went to college and got married two years later. Constance got married when she was thirty-five years old. They were all in each other's wedding. Coincidentally, they all have two children.

Teresa is always in search of the perfect gift to give everyone. Also, her main mission this year was to find the perfect Christmas tree. She insisted that Constance go looking with her. She stated she always helps Constance select gifts to buy for her family. Diane is the one that will buy a gift card or simply give money. The three of them do not exchange gifts. It has been a yearly tradition for them to get together during December to go to a movie, shopping or spend time dinning at what they consider to be a classy restaurant. They enjoy each other's company and can talk for hours.

Teresa appears to be the most gregarious of the three. She informs you she has always been a homemaker. Diane and Constance are professional women who continue to work outside of the home. You observed the closeness of the three friends. They tell you their friendship is very important to them. They enjoy their end of the year gathering because it sets the tone for the New Year. They always decide the location of their next three-day summer trip during this time of the year.

It is obvious these three women are very different in their perspectives about the holiday season, but they look forward to new beginnings as the old year-ends and the New Year starts. Best friends are a merry combination.

Deworn, giving in spirit, loyal in friendship

Some people you simply cannot say no to, as is the case with Deworn. She is very giving in spirit and to know her is to love her, although for some people this is not necessarily immediate. Nevertheless, she is deserving of praise and she is a loyal friend and confidant. Some of her best attributes are her willingness to openly display compassion, patience, and concern for others; especially during their time of bereavement. She has personally befriended many during their time of loss. In the process, she has motivated others to join her in aiding individuals coping with grief.

Deworn has been a loyal best friend over the past 30 years. Her generosity has always inspired you. When she asks for your assistance, you find it difficult to refuse her. She has that effect on most people. You have seen her spear head numerous functions to thank others and show them appreciation for their unselfishness in helping her reach out to others during their time of need.

As you watch Deworn in action at a recent event that she hosted to acknowledge her thanks to co-workers, past and present, you feel a sense of pride in knowing her as a best friend. Deworn does not believe in excuses. Her strong faith is an asset. She is always confident that you will find a way to accomplish what your heart desires. She is persistent and consistent. Her passion is impressive and contagious. She wants to do more than hold your hand and hug you as you face life's problems. She is an engaging person who openly and willingly displays genuine concern for others through numerous acts of kindness.

Your many years of friendship with Deworn have been filled with demonstrations of what encompasses true friendship. Honesty heads the list. You have learned to agree to disagree. You give each other space. The two of you have shared many personal moments. You have laughed together and cried together. Although you consider your best friend relationship with Deworn to be very special, you must also recognize that you are not alone in valuing her friendship. Her circle of friends is wide and impressive. Age, sex, race, nor financial status have proven to be a hindrance to her desire to reach out to others. You smile as you realize that Deworn has established a legacy of unselfish love.

Student, athlete, best friend

Eighteen years old Billy commands attention as he enters the classroom. He is 6' 1" tall with a slender build. He is currently a senior at Raleigh Egypt High School in Memphis, TN. He is also a star basketball and football player who acknowledges that he has a best friend.

Billy states his best friend, Tanner, also attends Raleigh Egypt High School. They both play football, but his best friend's other interest is baseball. They have been best friends for the past two years. They live near each other and enjoy just hanging out together. Billy reveals that they have the same mindset. He knows he can trust his best friend who "keeps it real".

Having a best friend who he feels is like a brother is very important to Billy. He states both of their parents feel that they have gain another son. He said they talk about their future a lot and they are looking at the possibility of attending the same college. As for now, they are both proud to be referred to as Raleigh Egypt Pharaohs. They met at their alma mater two years ago.

You found it interesting that Billy said being best friends involved just bonding. He obviously appreciates his best friend relationship. It is something very special to him. He made a point of pointing out his best friend who is also eighteen in a later class session. You could see how they acknowledged each other by their eye contact and body language. You picked up on differences in their personalities during class. Nevertheless, you could tell that they were content with who they were and they did not put on airs in each other's presence. You felt certain that this best friend relationship would deepen as the years passed by and they were going to always treasure this unique bonding.

The dynamics of male bonding has its own unique aspect that is somewhat different from women. You observed it being displayed in these two young men. The male pattern of friendship is not as physical or as emotional. Yet, you can still sense a very strong connection and closeness.

Fueled by common interests, mutual respect, and participation in shared activities a foundation has been laid that contributes to a lifelong best friend relationship.

What does a dog, a book, and a retired school teacher have in common?

What does a dog, a book, and a retired schoolteacher have in common? Let's read on.

"Outside of a dog, a book is man's best friend. Inside of a dog, it's too dark to read". This quote by Groucho Marx jumps out at you as you enter the Germantown Library on a Saturday morning. It was the reference to best friend that caught your attention. That is always significant.

You are at the library with one of your best friends. She is a retired schoolteacher and librarian. She is tutoring a young 13 years old male student. You drove them to the library. You have a lot of admiration for your best friend. The two of you met when you were a freshman in college. She was a junior. She has been the big sister that you never had. Your personalities are quite different. Sometimes, it is an enigma to you that the two of you have remain such close friends for the past 40 years.

You sequester yourself at a nearby reading booth after finding a book to read. You occasionally glance at how intense your best friend is as she interacts with the young student. She definitely appears to have his attention. You sense a bond developing between them. The crystallization of your friendship is made stronger as you and your best friend try to be available to come to the aid of this rather impressive young man. He is a star athlete at his school. Nevertheless, he is willing to sacrifice a Saturday morning to improve his reading skills. He deserves a high five and so does your best friend. She has never let you down.

You will not dispute Grouch Marx's statement that books and dogs are in the category of being a man's best friend. You also appreciate the diversity allowed in defining the word, best friend. It is an enduring term with many options. You opt to hold on to the human aspect as most significant.

In conclusion, the answer to the question at the beginning should be quite apparent. If not, it's okay to continue to enjoy frolicking with your dog, cuddling up with a good book, and hanging out with your bosom buddy. After all, that's what best friends are for.

Best friends attend documentary film: The Memphis 13

The line was very long as you arrived to attend the free showing of the documentary film, The Memphis 13. The parking lot at the Malco Paradiso was quite full although you arrived 35 minutes before starting time. You had been invited to attend this 6 :00 PM showing on Oct. 06, 2011 by a close associate. The large turnout was most impressive.

As you attempt to locate your friend, you suddenly realize that you are standing by a former co-worker who is waiting on a best friend to arrive. You conclude this is significant and found yourself noticing a lot of couples. Some were males, some were females, and some were mixed males and females. It was awesome to see so many young people in attendance and many of them were also in pairs.

You sat next to two middle school-aged girls. They did express some laughter during parts of the film that you found inappropriate. Nevertheless, you didn't want to be judgmental. After all, you were their age once and you most certainly recalled finding humor in matters that you should have taken more seriously. The girls did comment that they had homework to do. You were proud that the two youthful friends thought enough of the documentary to come to see it on a school night. The 45-minute documentary film by Memphis law professor, Daniel Kiel, dealt with the 13 black students who were chosen to integrate 4 elementary schools in 1961. Professor Kiel expressed a hope at the end of the film that it would generate more dialogue about the significance of the major role these young children played in the integration history of Memphis, Tennessee public schools. The current mayor of Memphis, A.C. Wharton, beautifully narrated the film.

You decided to call your best friend when you got home to discuss the film. You were totally unaware of this aspect in the history of public school integration in Memphis. Your friend said it was news to her as well. You both conclude it must have been a difficult choice for the parents to make considering the time period. You have to admire the courage of the 13 young black children. You found yourself making a personal commitment to share this historical revelation with your family, circle of friends and others that you encounter. You made the first move by calling your best friend.

A timely call from a best friend

It's been several months since you and your best friend had a lengthy conversation. When the phone rings on a Friday night at 7:13pm, you smile. It's your best friend. Evidently, you are on the same wavelength. You had been thinking about her and what a coincidence, she had you on her mind. You both have a good laugh about this.

Your best friend reminds you that in a few months you will be leaping into another age dimension. You think how uncanny. You had been giving that some thought as well. Turning fifty-nine is one year ahead of the big sixty. Your best friend has already passed that milestone. She tells you that unfortunately you will never catch up with her. She states she feels obligated to warn you that you are headed for a long stretch that will keep you reflecting on your past, present and future. But she insists that you must focus on where you are now and where you are headed.

You thought how great it is to have a friend who has a few years on you. You respect her knowledge base. She has shared so many interesting views about life. She is not afraid of the good, the bad, or ugliness that exists in this still wonderful world. She has taught you that everybody deserves the best that life has to offer. Do not be judgmental. Focus on being happy. Focus on that feel good feeling that evades so many people. It is okay to be adventuresome. You shared with her that sometimes when you dared yourself you scared yourself. She was always pounding in your head that you were in charge of your life. Of course, only in these past few years have you finally grasped the significance of this point.

You and your best friend have chosen different paths in life. You must admit that you have vicariously lived a lot of experiences through her. There were many times that you secretly envied her life style. Nevertheless, it was your best friend who helped you to be more accepting of yourself and of your life. She even shared with you that there were times she envied you. Life is full of surprises. Turning fifty-nine will allow you to shine as you become more refined. Most important of all, a call from a best friend is always timely.

Qualities of a best friend

Important qualities of a best friend vary depending on whom you talk to. The overall focus seems to embody enduring trust, honesty, and being supportive.

Ask a soon to be twenty nine year old female and you might be told that the trusted best friend knows when to speak and when to just listen. It is a special trait that makes them a valuable support base as you deal with the mundane problems of daily living. Because they are usually not within your immediate family circle, you appreciate sharing personal issues that you just need to sort through and hopefully resolve.

Make this same inquiry of a fifty-year-old male and he might reveal that best friends have your best interest at heart. If you want an honest opinion, ask a best friend. You have reached a plateau in your relationship where you can agree to disagree. Your best friend will be supportive. They will give you space and understand that it's okay to have quiet time away from everybody, including them.

The trusted best friend always has your back as expressed by several middle school students. They also added that best friends enjoy the same activities that you do. You can discuss confidential matters with them and they are not judgmental. They can remain objective. They allow you to be a real person.

The overall consensus revealed that best friends are about sharing and caring. Best friends are about giving and forgiving. Best friends are about fun and laughter. Best friends are about joy and happiness. Best friends are about kindness, thankfulness, and gratitude.

Most important it can be concluded that best friends are about honesty. They develop an unshakeable trust in each other that remains in place as the years pass. They have shared and experienced many memorable happenings going through life's corridors. They have always extended a helping hand to each other. Their special bond of trust is often a quiet confidence in the uniqueness and creative spirit of another individual. This strong positive bond also encompasses respect and loyalty that will always survive the storms of life as well as the passing of time.

A true No. 1 best friend

The wait for your ride on the Blueline Express while in Chicago gave you the opportunity to initiate conversation with one of the commuters. You felt she had a friendly smile. She confirmed that you were waiting on the right side to board the train for Bluemont.

Next, you asked the commuter if she had an interesting best friend story. She displayed a hesitant smile. She said yes but did not want to use personal names. You told her that was okay. She appeared to become more relaxed. As you both set on the bench waiting for the train, she related how she recently discovered that she was the second best friend to her neighbor of 10 years. She had always assumed that she held first place.

You thought that it was unusual to rank your best friends' status. You had several best friends but never ranked them. This was significant. You listened intently. She shared with you that her best friend had asked her to keep her mixed Chow dog, Siam, for a couple of days. When the best friend returned to pick up the dog, she thanked her and informed her that next to Siam she was her second best friend. She had watched almost enviously as her neighbor embraced Siam and he had licked her face excitedly.

She said the idea of being second place to a dog weighed heavily on her mind for several days. However, she concluded that best friends should always be supportive. Siam had no awareness of the special place that he held. She thought about the detailed instructions that her friend had given to take care of Siam. She also called each day to check on him. She assumed this was responsible pet owner behavior. After all, the dog has been a part of her neighbor's life for the last 12 years.

She also had to admit that Siam was a pretty smart dog. When she took him for his morning walks, she felt he was the best protection. He did not bark in the house. He watched the same TV shows that she did. He slept at the foot of her bed. He woke her up by pulling at the bed covers. He made her smile and kept her laughing. Siam was good company, but most significantly he was a true "No.1" best friend.

As a best friend recovers

As a best friend recovers from the never timely loss of a love one, you try not to attempt to define their daily mood. The passing years have taught you to empathize but not feel sorry for others. You have also learned not to worry about those you love.

Best friends are always trying to give you free realm to "do you". The death factor requires your best friend to wait until you are ready to stop suffering. The pain of the loss of a spouse will always remain, but you can still choose to be thankful and grateful for all the precious beauty that life offers to the living.

A best friend recognizes that you are trying to move on with your life as you struggle with your loss. There are no time restraints. You must unravel through all of the emotional bonds. There will be good moments of happy memories and conflicting moments of anguish as you move forward.

Your best friend believes in your goodness. They recognize your quiet inner strength. You are a fighter. You will never give up on life. You have been temporarily stumbled by one of life's eventualities. Nevertheless, the eternal and abundant positive energy of the universe is still there for you to claim. You have an incomparable soul and you are thankful for the God that created you.

As your best friend recovers, you realize that it is wonderful to be alive. But it is more magnificent to know the truth that the universe has no restraints. Even in the face of death, you are connected to the oneness of the universe and exposed to a greater opportunity to understand that as long as you allow yourself to continue to evolve you can still be happy as you focus on all the goodness and positive energy that still remains. After all, the beauty of creation never ends. It just gets better and better if you just let it be. As a friend, you should always be ready with a smile.

When your best friend attends "Rock Da City Concert" without you

On Saturday, August 20, 2011, the place to be was at the Rock DA City Concert in Memphis. To quote the words of one of the entertainers, "...even if I had to walk to Memphis" I was going to be there. Your best friend was too busy and said she needed a more advanced notice. She has known you long enough to know that is how you operate sometimes.

Now your best friend is calling you wanting to know how did you enjoy the show. Well first of all dear friend, you really should have been there. When Michael Jackson appeared as the opening act, the audience just screamed uncontrollably. You found yourself shouting, "Unbelievable!!" Of course it is widely reported that Michael is dead, but it must be said that his spirit definitely lives on in the person of Nathan Davis. The mesmerizing Lesa G & the dynamic MT4 Band also rocked the house. Jazz Artist, Ms. BB captivated the audience with her gorgeous and sensuous appearance as well as with her beautiful vocal chords. Blues Artist, Jewel J was soulfully enticing and had the moves that made you want to groove. The overall diversity of the artists blended harmoniously as their unmistakable talents held the audience attention at all times. Sir Cedric and his band definitely made the audience want to dance. Rap Artist, Yung Nawledge made you listen more intensely. Booker Brown was passionate and soothing as he kept the audience moving with his soulful southern blues music.

Sweet Angel was the recipient of the Rock Da City 2011 Award. Her incomparable soulful sounds are unique and riveting. Her stage presence is most captivating. She is gracious and vivacious. You felt honored to be present at this first annual Rock the City Concert. In the meanwhile, you will try to keep up with future performances of some of the other impressive stars that graced the stage including, Bertha Payne, Misti Blu, A'prail Monique, Melodic, and Lachelle Rea. AJE Dreamland was a major sponsor in this production.

Of course, EZ Street summed it all up with his words, ". . . even if I had to walk to Memphis". Personally, you would not have missed this event held at the Bartlett Municipal Center located at the Memphis/Bartlett borderline. What's interesting is the fact that you could have actually walked to the function from your home.

Qualities of a best friend include your cheapest therapist

The assignment for the class involved writing about qualities of a best friend. You conclude this is going to be an easy task for this group of 8th graders.

However, as you walked around checking on their progress, most of them had an incomplete first sentence. A few students had only written their name on their paper.

Suddenly, one male student stated he did not have a best friend. A female student asked what did the word quality mean. You were pleased that another student responded appropriately with a correct definition and some examples as well. You walked over to check her paper. She had written one sentence. You sensed there was definitely a missing link to this assignment. You decided to have a brief classroom discussion. You wanted them to think outside the box.

You could not imagine being in the eighth grade and not having a best friend. You revealed you still had childhood best friends. Someone boldly asked how old were you. You stated you would let them figure that out.

Trying to stay on task, you asked if anyone had a pet that could be considered their best friend. No one confirmed that. You noted that a parent, sibling, or other relative could be considered a best friend. Someone said a cousin was their best friend. You breathed a sigh of relief. Another child said she had a best friend since she was four years old. Someone said a teacher could be a best friend. You nodded an affirmative yes. A comment was made that a fish could be a best friend. You said it was possible. You interjected an inanimate object such as a stuffed toy could be considered a best friend. No one followed up on that thought. You finally informed them to just consider what qualities would be important to them if they had a best friend. One student shouted out just pretend you have a best friend.

You were able to read several papers. You were relieved to see that best friends were still fun to be with and enjoyed doing the same things that you did. You could also tell them secrets. They were kind, trusting and thoughtful.

Your hope was that each of them would one day have a best friend as they ventured out into a challenging world and realized that "a best friend is cheaper than therapy". ★

★Author unknown

Best friend goes to Chicago meets Mazen, best friend of fashion

You are very excited when your best friend calls you and tells you after two days in Chicago she must return in the near future. You try not to be envious. After all, this is your best friend. She proceeds to tell you that she is touring all areas of the Windy City. She also mentions she has just bought her first pair of Babyphat jeans with the neatest matching Babyphat blouse at a great price. She bought her outfit at Mister Kay. The owner, Mazen, told her he recently did a fashion show in Memphis. This impressed her. She was able to get her jeans hemmed while she continued to visit other shops along this stretch of 87th Street.

You have not been to Chicago. The enthusiasm of your best friend makes you more determine to visit. You listen more intently as she tells you how pleased she was with the professional hemming of her jeans. They were a good fit, feel, and style. The personal attention of the staff in helping her choose the right pair of jeans was appreciated by her. She wore her outfit that evening to a function at the Rosemont Hyatt. She stated she received several compliments about her attire and proudly proclaimed Mazen to be a best friend of fashion. After all, at 58 years old she did have some minor reservations about the flattering and sexy outfit.

She stated she commuted by way of the Chicago Blueline Subway train to the Hyatt/Rosemont. This was also another first for her. Your best friend continued to call you with updates about what she was doing and viewing. You actually found yourself getting caught up in the excitement of the trip. You were already planning to visit Lakeshore Drive, the White Sox and the Bulls Stadiums, Garrett's Popcorn Store, Michigan Avenue, and Oprah's Studio. She even saw a side view of President Obama's home in Hyde Park.

Since you liked your best friend's taste in clothing, you would definitely find your way to Mr. Kay's Fine European Clothing Store. Your petite size would require some alterations. You couldn't wait to see your best friend's outfit. Perhaps you would meet Mazen.

Vicariously for you and in actuality for your best friend, Chicago was an amazing city of fun, fashion, fine dining and the latest happenings.

Memphis Finest to the rescue/Best friend proclaims Dir. Toney Armstrong as hero

It is Friday morning and you are sitting in the office of Toney Armstrong, the Director of the City of Memphis Police Department. He epitomizes Memphis Finest at its highest level and for your best friend he was proclaimed to be a hero. You were invited as moral support by your best friend to attend this meeting in the director's office.

This encounter was most significant in view of the solutions that were offered by Director Armstrong. Your best friend has been dealing with a fifteen year old civil matter that was escalating. Feeling somewhat desperate at this time, she felt that her only recourse was to have a personal audience with the City of Memphis Police Director to address her concerns. She was elated when she was given an appointment to meet with him today, July 21, 2011 at 10:00 A.M.

You observed how Director Armstrong showed empathy and patience with your friend. He let her know at the very beginning that it was his intention to offer a viable solution to the unfortunate matter that now brought her to his office. He was attentive and responded appropriately. He was able to give your best friend a feeling of relief as he explained the steps that would be taken to address her concerns.

The opportunity to observe the Director of Police take time out of his busy schedule to assist your best friend was revealing. Director Armstrong is to be commended for first of all being approachable. He was able to put your best friend at ease. You did not feel that he was being patronizing. The actions that he stated that would be taken to resolve her problems were most impressive. His professionalism was very apparent.

As the meeting came to an end, you noticed how your best friend displayed a genuine smile because she felt finally her concerns would be given the proper attention. Her sudden expression that Director Armstrong could be labeled her hero confirmed your conclusion that the meeting was a success. You even felt a sense of amelioration about the outcome and thought this was an excellent demonstration of Memphis Finest to the rescue.

You conclude best friends are also available to rescue you if it becomes necessary. Today, it was not necessary.

Best friends believe laughter is the best medicine

Best friends agree laughter is the best medicine. A smile is the generic twin and "Now" is the time to let the healing begin. So it was for best friends, Lee, Ruth and Maxine. They reunited in Atlanta, Ga. Ruth currently lives there. These three ladies with Memphis, TN roots concluded life is too short to abort because of the aging factor. There was so much chatter and laughter as they reminisced about the past. Recently, four exciting days together proved to be a very enjoyable as well as a very memorable time for them.

Lee and Maxine flew to Atlanta by way of Delta Airlines. Leaving out on July 02, 2011, the two had a fun flight after meeting Andy, their third seatmate. The effervescent and very friendly Maxine struck up conversation with him as soon as they settled in their seats. Lee was prepared to read during the flight, but found herself amused by the engaging conversation of her two seatmates. This was the beginning of an enjoyable and very pleasant trip. Ruth was the perfect hostess. Southern hospitality was the special daily charm along with good food and exciting things to do.

Of course, Memphis has its exciting tourists attractions. Nevertheless, Atlanta is most impressive. The shopping trip to Lenox Mall resulted in some good bargains. The trip to Farmer's Market was most interesting. Alon was a fun place to eat health food and Stone Mountain was amazing. The 4th of July laser celebration was phenomenal despite some light rain. Jimmy Carter's museum and garden most be revisited.

Seating on the back porch deck at Ruth's home and sipping Margarita's each night was the most fun of all as conversation flowed and topics varied. Their 40 years plus friendship provided a backdrop of genuine love and honesty. The return trip home came too soon. However, this brief encounter cemented their friendship on a more spiritual level. Their mutual respect for each other and total acceptance of each other's idiosyncrasies was very apparent. These three individuals have entered the golden years of their friendship and their lives are more enriched. They realize life is too short to abort despite aging. They are grateful and thankful for the simple blessings that life offers. They cherish the joy and laughter that long time best friendship provides.

Springtime and best friends year round

You are best friends year round, but springtime in Memphis, TN allows best friends to join in recapturing a renewed energy for life. They plan more fun and exciting things to do all over the city. They feel good about their beautiful town as they stroll through parks, malls and down by the river. Springtime is also revealing and teaches a lot about human nature. It is a time of growth and of positive transitioning. Best friends spring forth on what can be described as a new wave of positive energy and receive the abundance of the universe. They are in tune with nature and their soul.

Spring is also a time for best friends to re-examine what really matters in life. You feel revitalized and in control of your destiny. Your discussions are more metaphysical. You recognize that everything about life is a learning experience. You dig deeper into the meaning of your friendship. You appreciate the kindred spirit that you share. You plant new seeds of appreciation for all the things in life that really matter. You look forward with great anticipation to seeing each other bloom throughout the year. You will water and nourish each other. The main ingredients are caring, sharing, understanding and patience.

Best friends are close but grow at their own pace and its okay. They are not in a race. The time-space reality that allowed their paths to cross is infinite. Watching Ophra Winfrey highlight her friendship with her best friend, Gayle King, on TV recently confirmed this. You were especially impressed with the favorable comments about Gayle expressed by Stedman. It is admirable when you can have a significant other in your life who is not threatened by your best friend relationship. Ophrah is fortunate to have the best of both, a true best friend relationship and a wonderful and understanding male companion who loves her very much.

The dynamics of this trio's interaction epitomizes that true love is not selfish. Gayle was on the scene before Stedman and obviously neither was intimidated by the other. Both were able to share Ophra and graciously embrace each other. They realized the diverse roles they played as a part of Ophrah's life. Ophra as the common denominator impacted both their lives in a positive way. They are value players. Their paths have crossed. They are the best of friends year round.

Sweet sixteen, twins and best friends

Twins are always interesting you think as you call the classroom roll and realize you have a set of twin female students. The only way you can tell them apart is because they have on different colors. They have the same hairstyle; the same smile and their eyes even have the same sparkle in them. Their demeanor is pleasant. When you find a brief break, the two come to your desk and agree to talk with you about being twins and best friends.

The girls are sixteen years old identical twins and confirm they are best friends. They are tenth grade students at Manassas High School in Memphis, TN. They are the only children of their mother who they reported was thirty-seven years old when they were born. They both acknowledge they are very close to their mother who has no difficulty telling them apart. They informed you that their birthmarks were on different parts of their body.

It is obvious that the twins have similar personalities. They share an interest in music, are band students and play the clarinet. Their long-term vocational objectives involve careers in the medical field; one aspired to be a doctor and the other a nurse.

As twins, they shared the same room until they were twelve years old. They noted it was an adjustment for them to be separated; adding they still occasionally slept together. The twin who was delivered first considered herself to be the older big sister. You could detect a protective attitude as she interacted with her "younger" sister. The most fascinating thing you observed was how they would display certain movements simultaneously. Indeed, they did act alike, laughed alike, and talked alike.

Being twins had many advantages. The girls were very popular. In addition, they were attractive and smart. It is apparent these two young ladies will always be there for each other. Their close bond obviously began in their mother's womb. They stated their closeness was just natural for them. You observed how they often looked directly at each other and smiled. You felt as though they were communicating telepathically. Their best friend bond was of a superlative nature. It felt good to be in their presence. You realized that you were observing a strong spiritual and unconditional love on a level that single birth individuals rarely experienced.

Carol Barnett, full of determination and a student's best friend

Do not let her endearing smile and small petite stature fool you. Carol Barnett is a woman on fire. She is a woman on a mission and she is tenacious. She is determined and most of all she is deserving of being labeled a student's best friend. Her zeal and unrelenting determination to improve the academic status, intellectual and social exposure of advanced students in the Memphis School system has not gone unnoticed. Her recognition that there are many deserving students who dare to dream of post high school educational and professional pursuits that extend beyond neighborhood boundaries deserves special acknowledgement.

On March 27, 2011, Carol was honored as a recipient of the Women of Achievement Award. The Mistress of Ceremonies was Ursula Madden of Channel Five News. Carol Barnett's presenter was Miska Shaw, a Memphis Prep Alumnae and now an attorney residing in Memphis.

The ceremony was inspiring. Carol was one of seven women who have demonstrated willingness and a commitment to advocate unselfishly for a cause that has resulted in a benefit to individuals as well as entire communities.

Carol was cited for her "Determination" to assist as many high performing students as possible to move forward beyond their comfort zones. The students were encouraged to take the plunge into new educational challenges by attending summer prep programs at prestigious schools all over the country. Carol was instrumental in keeping the goals of the original summer prep school program alive. This program started with the vision of Jed Dreifus, Frances Hooks and several others. Beginning with only one student, each passing year the numbers slowly increased and the number of schools expanded. Thanks to Carol's involvement the Memphis Prep Program moved forward at an unprecedented pace. A small number of one has now increased to over one hundred students in one summer being able to continue in the pursuit of learning and growing in knowledge.

Upon their return home, many students display an attitude of gratitude. Their future is brighter as they come to the realization that they can believe and achieve and gladly receive the best that life has to offer them.

Carol Barnett has demonstrated that she is a caring and generous best friend with determination. Her sincere and steadfast loyalty to improve the future of youths in the community has sparked a fire that can never be extinguished

When your best friend is a shopaholic

It is a cool spring morning. You are comfortably sleeping in your bed between micro fiber sheets covered with a blanket and a quilt. You found the queen size sheet set at a bargain price at Marshall's. You are feeling proud of yourself. Suddenly the ringing of your cell phone interrupts your thoughts. That ring tone belongs to your best friend. No one else would have the nerve to call you before 6:00 in the morning.

Your best friend is very excited. She has mapped out a plan of four stores to shop at before 12 noon. You have confronted your best friend several times about being a shopaholic. She refuses to admit it. As she tells you excitedly that she also has shopping plans for the entire day, you recognize that over the years you have played the role of an enabler. You often accompany her on shopping excursions. You recall a few weeks ago that you were the one who told her about the micro fiber sheets you found at Marshall's. Now your best friend has four sets. You only have one. She was able to find the sheet sets in the full sizes and one king size. Yes she bought the king size. She will give the king set as a gift in the future. The $19.99 price was a good deal!

You find yourself trying to get excited about an early morning shopping excursion. You decide you need to accompany your best friend to make sure that she doesn't over indulge. She has an obsessive-compulsive tendency to buy several of the same items on sale. Her kitchen pantry is like a mini store. She stocks up on everything. Sam's has contributed significantly to her shopping frenzies. You made the mistake of telling her to sign up for a Sam's card. She loves the store and never comes out empty handed. You also exposed her to some of Memphis' thrift stores, thinking she could save money. Now she shops at all her regular stores and then makes a last minute visit to a thrift store.

You smile as you get up out of bed to do your morning exercise before joining your best friend. You wonder what good bargains will you find. You conclude when your best friend is a shopaholic it can be a good thing.

Best friend relationships, simple and free

The best things in life are simple and free. This is a very significant point when looking at the dynamics of a best friend relationship. Best friends are truthful, loving and giving. They do not sympathize with you. They empathize with you. There is a difference. They know how to be positive with you no matter how dismal circumstances can appear. They enjoy seeing you transform your dreams into realities and you feel the same for them.

Best friends give freely and unconditionally. They do not worry about you because they love you. They know that you are a good person with good intentions. They give you space and let you know that they are always available. They are not judgmental. They are forgiving.

Best friends will surprise you and send you a greeting card to let you know that they are just thinking about you. They are fortunately just "a phone call away, a text message away, or an E-mail away, and a thought away". It is not about needing them. They just want to let you know they care about you. Best friends know how to make you smile.

Best friends will invite you to see the play, "A Raisin in the Sun" at the Collierville Harrell Theatre put on by Memphis' outstanding performers with Hattieloo's Theatre. They will pick you up and suggest you go out to eat after the play ends. You find yourself at Buckley's Fine Filet Grill. It was your first time dining at Buckley's. To your delight, the food, the atmosphere and the service were impressive. Being in the company of your best friend made it more pleasant.

Best friends freely reach out to each other. They realize the great value in having such a special bond. They are aware that there is a spiritual energy that they share. A best friend relationship is significant. It adds a special dimension that enhances the quality of your life at no cost. It is simply a mutual appreciation of the uniqueness of another individual's goodness and kindness. It is not conditional, nor contingent upon anything. It is one of life's simple and free provisions. We can tap into this energy as early as young infants or later in our adult life. This mutual love and respect originates from the heart.

Best friends are terrific/best friends are champions

You are an adult observer in Incredible Pizza. It is noisy with the sounds of music, vending machines and children's merriment. You fixate on two four years old embracing. They are excited to see each other. You smile. You realize it is the beginning of the beginning. The foundation of a best friend relationship is being laid. You hope there will be no interference. Their youthful innocence is very apparent. They continue to hold hand after embracing. You listen as the seemingly more assertive and protective one lovingly tells her companion that she will go with her to spin the big wheel. The two walk toward the big wheel. You see the growing confidence in the one who had been hesitant.

You find yourself reflecting back on memories of childhood best friends. A feel good emotion emerges as you begin to recall some past experiences. One notably one was when you were in the play, Cinderella, with your best friend. She was chosen by your favorite teacher to play the role of Cinderella. You were very excited for her. She had been nervous about the role but you just knew she would be good for the part. That was second grade. Your families moved soon after that and you lost contact with each other.

Remembering your best friend's full name, you pondered over trying to locate her. You will give it more thought. Perhaps she still lives in Memphis.

Suddenly, your regression down memory lane is interrupted by the sound of very loud laughter. It is the two young girls. They are now running and skipping about. The spinning wheel challenge was met. This is the victory celebration. Having a best friend is terrific! They are both champions!!!

Best friendship beginning:
A Memphis/Boston connection

The beginning of a beautiful friendship is kindred to walking alone into a crowded room. You feel apprehensive. You do not see a familiar face. Suddenly, as your eyes repeatedly scan the room you look into the face of someone who smiles and you smile back. It is a feeling of relief.

Sitting on the bed in your cruise cabinet, you have last minute jitters. You decided to share a cabinet room. You had no control over who your roommate would be. Yes, it would be a female, but that is all the data that was available. You boarded the ship first. You are trying to feel excited about the cruise and not dwell on what your roommate would be like. You decide that you like the room. You conclude that the bedding will have to be rearranged. The room is set up for a couple. You visually select which side of the room you prefer. You are elated that you had an outside room with a porthole window. Suddenly, you are aware that the door to the room is opening. Now, your primary concern was that the two of you would be compatible and you hoped that she did not snore.

You remain quiet as the door opened wider. The smiling face that entered the room immediately gave you a feeling of relief. You decided it was the beginning of a beautiful friendship. As a matter of fact, by the end of the cruise you decided it was the beginning of a beautiful best friend relationship. Not only were the two of you compatible, there was no snoring. You slept like a baby all three nights. Your days were a delight. You enjoyed the food, the weather, the seminars and the company of your new friend from Boston, Mass. You became inseparable. She liked your southern Memphis, TN charm. You liked her Trinidad/Boston charm. Your new friend even convinced you to stay up late one evening and enjoy a night of dancing. You were caught up in the merriment. No drinking. Just fun. Your tired feet eventually demanded rest. Still, you and your roommate woke up excited and alert about the start of a new day.

The beginning of a friendship is a beautiful experience. It is one of those happenings that make life terrific as seen in this Memphis/ Boston connection. Two champions meet. Life is grand!

Best friends everywhere in Memphis

There is a Best Friends Forever (BFF) invasion in Memphis, TN. They can be spotted everywhere. Their main hang out is on Beale Street, a concentrated entertainment Mecca with a host of restaurants, clubs, stores and shops. Just try strolling up and down this tourist stretch on weekends. You will find yourself stumbling all over them. You don't need a radar to detect them. Their smiling faces give them away. Do not go there if you are not in the mood for smiling and having fun. The BFFs will lure you in. They are locals and visitors from all over the world. Some will stop and tell you that they visited Elvis Presley's Graceland Mansion. They are usually easily to detect because they will often say, "I got on my blue suede shoes." Try not to look too conspicuously at their feet. On the other hand, if they say Elvis gave them a tour, quickly walk away from them.

Many locals while dinning in Lil Anthony's-Café with their best friends are often approached by the friendly visiting BFFs who are very excited and decided to remain in Memphis longer than planned. They invite themselves to sit at your table as they call other BFFs on their cell phones to come to Memphis. You smile and make room for them.

Best friends enjoy cold weather

Best friends enjoy all kinds of weather. They will plan a trip to the Bahamas in February and return to their hometown of Memphis still in a good mood despite temperatures in the thirties. Best friends wake up every morning ready to chat before the day begins. They encourage one another to have a great day especially when it is bone chilling cold.

The cold weather that has been lingering in Memphis has made best friends more determined to have a terrific day. Dinner at Rafferty's is one of their special hangouts. It does not matter if it is just the two of them, or if others join them. They understand the special warmth that they both share. Their lives are about living in the "NOW" moment and moving forward. They are fortunate to have bonded in a way that no day will be so cold that they feel immobilized. The cold for them is about carrying on life's dreams. Dreams were made for all kinds of weather.

Best friends help one another through life's unexpected storms. They will lift you up from cold gripping claws due to the loss of a loved one and help you see that it is okay to smile and feel the warm blood that runs through you. They help you understand your life will get better.

Overall, best friends enjoy cold weather together because they simply enjoy life. They radiate natural warmth that propels them to never allow the weather to determine how their days go. In conclusion, best friends always enjoy cold weather with a warm smile and a sunny disposition.

Best friends feel you

You can't hide your true feelings from a best friend. To borrow a common cliché, "They read you like a book". It's an intuitive trait that is a part of the kindred spirit that you share. The best friend bond has a dimension that unites individuals in a way that defies verbal explanations. This invisible connection is very real as exhibited by the need to always be there for one another no matter how far away and no matter how personal a matter might be. Even though you live in Memphis, Tn, your best friend will come running as close as across town or as far away as Texas, California or Georgia.

Best friends are not there to judge, qualify or quantify what you do. You owe them no explanations. They simply feel you. They want you to be happy.

Best friends feed off each other's vibes. They are willing to share each other's joy and pain. Like a protective mother hen, they will surround you with their love and be there to protect you. Best friends allow you to continue to evolve and want more of the wonderful things that life has to offer. When you fall down or simply slow down, best friends are there to pick you up and help you maintain your momentum. They constantly remind you that there is no need for you to struggle, especially alone.

Best friends are there as you reach milestones in life. They are there to comfort you as you cope with the death on a spouse. They share your joy when you become a grandparent. They are your cheering squad as you accomplish your goals. They don't mind growing old with you and hanging out at Perkins Restaurant for breakfast and Texas Longhorn Restaurant for dinner.

Most important of all, best friends are about each other's well-being. They help you realize that you are beautiful person. You feed on each other's positive energy. Best friends bring each other relief. Best friends feel you.

State of TN Co-workers, a broad spectrum of best friends

In the realm of best friend relationships, the work place provides a broad spectrum for individuals to establish lasting bonds. Co-workers often develop cohesiveness as they continue to work together to provide quality services for their employers and the customers that utilize their services. The bond that is forged as a result of being in this environment is often subtle. Eventually, this constant interaction develops a personal aspect. A close camaraderie relationship surfaces. An unspoken commitment to look out for each other and to assure the work unit is operating at maximum capacity with or without direct supervisory presence takes hold.

This phenomenon has as its basis a mutual and genuine interest in the life of their fellow co-worker that often extends beyond the work site. As time passes, the closeness evolves into a best friend status. There is a need to be a continuous part of each other's life. You are keenly aware of the love, respect and personal concern that unite them together.

There is also a nurturing and protective perspective to a best friend relationship that is established on the job. It is usually two-fold. It exists on the job and outside the job. A level is reached that equates to a family of best friends. You work together and you socialize together. You laugh together and you cry together as life's eventualities happen. The end result is that the best friend bond is made stronger by these occurrences.

Best friend relationships are constantly expanding. Co-worker relationships that develop into close or best friend relationships are happening every day. Not everyone is in this unique position. For those who are, their lives are enriched. They have a strong network of support outside the traditional family framework. You conclude living the majority of your life in Memphis, TN. and working for the local Department of Human Services was a goldmine for finding lasting friendships. State employees are champions when it comes to being supportive when one of their own, current or former co-workers, suddenly finds themselves in need of comfort.

Memphis' Finest, Public Servants, Best Friend

As public servants, Memphis' Finest★, the City of Memphis Police Department is always there to serve and protect. They are also there to serve as your best friend. Never let it be said that the City of Memphis Police Department does not support the family of one of their own. Memphis' Finest opens a floodgate of loving concern and active support. They represent the full spectrum of "we are here if you need us" and "know that you are not alone". The entire department epitomizes the compassion of a best friend.

Memphis' Finest is not about talk when one of their own dies. They are about action. The death of one of their own under any circumstance is not taken lightly. The supportive best friend mode surfaces like a raging bull. They are always there to serve and protect; now they are ready to extend loving and protective arms. Like a true best friend, they let you know that they are personally there to see you through every step of the way during your hour of bereavement.

The loss of one of Memphis' Finest triggers an outpouring of genuine care for the surviving family. Just as best friends instinctively know what you need, Memphis' Finest provides a network of loving support and encouragement.

It will take time to heal from the loss of a loved one. However, you are in a unique position when that loved one was one of Memphis' Finest. You will have a plethora of best friends who will always support you and extend a helping hand.

The City of Memphis Police deserves special recognition and appreciation for their role in displaying a united front. They are an exceptional brotherhood. They are a family of public servants committed to serving and protecting, especially one of own. They extend their bond to include entire families in the event of the loss of one of their fellow members.

They are the unsung best friends of their fellow colleague's family as well as the community.

★ One of Memphis' Finest, Major Charlie G. Gordon, passed on Oct. 16, 10 and was funeralized Oct. 23, 10 at Hill Chapel Baptist Church in Memphis, TN. Without question, the City of Memphis Police Department stepped up to the plate and assisted his family through a difficult time displaying the loving and genuine manner of a loyal best friend.

Best friend meets friendly stranger

Traveling to Dallas, Texas via Greyhound can be an interesting trip. You think perhaps it might lead to the start of a new best friend relationship. You board the bus in downtown Memphis. You feel a nervous excitement. You look for a vacant seat toward the middle section. The only friendly face that you observe is of a young white male, possibly thirty-ish. He's seating at the window seat. He attempts to allow more room for you and offers to put your carry-on bag in the overhead storage area. As he does so, you conclude he's got to be at least six feet tall.

You engage in some polite conversation. He reveals that he is headed for California. He stopped in Memphis to visit some friends in Cordova. He caught a cab from Cordova to the bus station. He tells you that he is going to surprise his parents. They have no idea he is coming. You think how nice. He states he might stick around if the job market looks promising.

You are being very cautious. You think you don't want to reveal too much. It is a night trip. Your seatmate doses off to sleep intermittently and surprisingly he does not snore. You found that to be very unusual.

Your seatmate had food to snack on and politely offered you some during the ride. You refused, thinking how nice of him to offer. He tells you he has grown a lot since being away from his parents and can appreciate them more. He has a better understanding of life since he has been on his own. You begin to calm down even more about your seatmate. You find yourself feeling a motherly connection toward him.

The bus makes several stops before arriving in Dallas. You are able to get a good look at your seatmate as you get off and on. You conclude there is a youthful and handsome ruggedness to his looks.

You remain awake the entire ride to Dallas. You didn't meet a best friend on the trip, but you did enjoy talking to a friendly stranger. As he walks away, you recall he used his cell phone several times during the bus ride. Perhaps he was talking to a best friend. You hope he has a happy reunion with his parents.

You decide to call your best friend and tell her about your trip.

Best friends re-connect

A surprise visit from one of your best friends is always a welcome one. The unexpected visit is indicative of her spontaneity. That is what you love about her. She was always more adventurous than you.

Your best friend flew in from Boston. She informs you that she is a six months divorcee. The settlement left her financially secure, but emotionally drained. She decided it was time to go on a spending spree. Naturally, she thought of you. It didn't matter that you had lost touch with her about 3 years ago. You recall the last time you spoke by phone she was in Las Vegas, Nevada and she was not married. Perhaps she got caught up in the Las Vegas life style. You wonder if she had a Las Vegas quick divorce. You'll get the details later.

Your best friend insists that you meet her at the Peabody for breakfast. She takes care of the tab. As a matter of fact, you spend the entire day together and she also pays for lunch and dinner. After breakfast, you take her to several shops on South Main Street. Next, you head out to Collierville Mall. You drive. She likes the Dillard's Store. She buys one outfit and two pairs of shoes. She insists on buying you a purse that you were admiring. You try to refuse, but she is persistent. Then she tells you she is going to New York City after leaving Memphis. She invites you. You tell her the timing is not good. You will plan to visit her in Boston in the spring. She seems pleased.

Reconnecting with your best friend made you realize how much you missed her. She was always a free spirit. You conclude that being opposites is what attracted you to each other. Your bond is still strong. You tell her you hope to hear from her more often. After all, the clock is ticking very fast and three years is a long time for two middle age prima donnas. Your best friend smiles. She tells you she was thinking the exact same thing.

B.B.Kings Blues Club and the smiling lady at the bar equate to southern hospitality for best friends

It is a Thursday night. You and your best friend decide to check out Ms. Ruby Wilson at B.B. King's Blues Club on Beale Street in Memphis. You make your entry. You are impressed with the live band's music on the ground floor.

Climbing up the stairs to the Upper Room, you are immediately caught up in the relaxing and calming ambiance. People are laughing, talking, standing, sitting, eating and drinking. They are grouped in twos, threes and more. They are young, middle aged and possibly older. You conclude they are enjoying each other's company and having a really good time.

Ms. Ruby is sitting by the piano near the top of the stair's entrance. You and your best friend greet her. She is pleased to see that you came. Your eyes gradually begin to adjust to the dim lighting of the room. You scope out where you want to sit. You both agree on the bar area near Ms. Ruby. That was a good choice. You are immediately given a taste of southern hospitality. Sitting at the bar is a stylish and attractive lady who tells you her name. She initiates friendly conversation and introduces you to her two friends at the bar. They are also there in support of Ms. Ruby. Your new friend reveals they have reserved a table. She invites you to join them. They are also waiting on several more friends to arrive.

As you move to the reserved table area, the blue tinted windows give the room a surreal effect as you look out over Beale Street. You enjoy engaging conversation with your new acquaintances. Their other friends begin to trickle in. The more the merrier definitely applies here. Your table group is lively.

It turned out to be a very fun evening. You and your best friend agreed it was an unexpected treat to meet the lovely and amicable lady at the bar.

Her friends were also very personable and pleasant. You cannot help but smile as you think hanging out on Beale Street is probably the best way to get a taste of friendly southern hospitality. B.B. King's Blues Club is a good starting point. Perhaps you might run into another affable lady at the bar and be captivated by her friendly smile.

On the ride home, you smile as you conclude going out with a best friend is rewarding.

A best friend's challenge:
Are you smarter than a fifth grader?

"Are you smarter than a fifth grader?" can become a real challenge when you dare yourself to sit down and eat lunch with them. This challenge is even more daring if the location is at Raleigh Bartlett Meadows Elementary School in Memphis, TN.

Conversations at the lunch table can be quite interesting. Some might revolve around you. Be prepared to be asked if you are a classmate's grandmother, even though it was established in class that morning that you are the substitute teacher for the day. So you smile when the student sitting across the table from you asks cautiously if you really are the grandmother of the student sitting next to you on your right. You turn and take a good look at the rather handsome young man who is being fidgety and avoids giving you eye contact. You realize this is a very delicate matter. Being the smart adult, your response is that you are for that day. Then you quickly change the topic. You ask if they consider their mother or father to be their best friend. One quickly queries, "How can your mother be your best friend?" . . . It must be a macho thing. The one sitting next to you grins and states his father is his best friend. The other one nods his head in agreement and adds that his father bought him an X-box from Toys R Us. Not to be out done, your grandson for the day states his father took him to the skating rink. To avoid this conversation becoming a contest for the best father, you promptly question if they were named after their fathers. One immediately raises his hand as though in the classroom and proudly says, "Me!" The one who happens to be the grandson for the day bows his head and says, "No." While you debate how to continue with this conversation, after all he is your grandson for the day, he suddenly looks defiantly at the student across the table. He pompously utters, "My mom tells me I look and act just like my father."

You breathe a sigh of relief. You are very proud of your grandson for the day. Obviously, he is quite cerebral. You quietly accept that perhaps you are not as smart as a fifth grader and wonder why fathers get more recognition as being best friends.

A former next door neighbor, a life time best friend

Imagine growing up next door to your best friend. Combine this with the fact that your parents were friends and neighbors before you were born. In this case, not only do you and your best friend establish a relationship that endures into your adult life, but also your entire family and your best friend's family have a very strong bond. This is definitely a real life saga of two neighboring families that should be produced on TV. These two intact Black families each have six girls and one boy. The setting is Benford Street in South Memphis. Family tragedies and triumphs over the years have served to draw them closer together. Sit down with Gwendolyn Bowman Watkins and Katie Nailey Wilkerson to get the unbelievable history of their lasting friendship.

Owen Brennan's Restaurant is the location of this most interesting revelation. You listen with fascination as you enjoy the early morning brunch. You manage to take a few breaks from the details of their closely intertwined lives to try the bread pudding on the buffet and found it to be simply wonderful to your palate. You're enjoying the live music in the background. Gwen and Katie reveal to you that the jazz saxophonist, Lanny McMillan, Jr, grew up on Benford Street as well.

The connection that these two best friends share is remarkable. Gwen continues to reside in Memphis, TN. She is a supervisor with the US Post Office in Bartlett, TN. Katie lives in Inglewood, CA. and is employed as a Customer Service Representative with See's Candies. Despite the long distance between them, Gwen and Katie continue to stay in touch almost weekly by phone. Katie has made numerous return trips to her hometown of Memphis. Sometimes she stays with Gwen instead of family. Coincidentally, Katie and Gwen each have one child. Katie has a very beautiful adult daughter named, Shelia. Gwen has a very handsome adult son, affectionately called "Dee". Their children are also developing a close friendship. In conclusion, it must be said that there is nothing imaginary about this best friend relationship. Without hesitation, it must be noted that this most enduring friendship just gets better with time.

And the "BFF" Award goes to Kimberly Carter and LaRosa Parks

Have you ever been excited about interviewing celebrities? Then, read further. You are about to be introduced to two recipients, Kimberly Carter and LaRosa Parks, of the BFF (BEST Friend Forever) Award.★ Join them in Kimberly's office. Allow yourself to get caught up in the positive energy that they share. Join in the laughter as they tell you how they met. You are captivated by the invisible, yet very apparent chemistry that they share.

Kim and LaRosa's BFF legacy scans over 18 years. You listen with fascination as they share the many things they have in common. They were both born in the same year. Both are married to wonderful husbands in law enforcement. Both are supervisors employed by the State of TN. They live about 5 minutes from each other. They attend the same church. E. Lynn Harris is their favorite author. They love to dine at the Olive Gardens. Cellular South handles their cell phone accounts. And, there is more. They look alike, talk alike and act alike. What unique friends!

Kim and LaRosa revealed that they talk to each other every single day. Their chance encounter was based on the drawing power of laughter. Kim often heard LaRosa's laughter in the office and finally decided she had to meet the person behind the laughter. That decision established the foundation for a friendship based on mutual similarities, interests, trust, respect and laughter. As a result, two families have bonded together.

There are no unknown variables in this relationship. To be in their presence and hear their contagious laughter reveals all the answers to the equation, "What adds up to a best friend?" There is obviously an exponential component to their closeness that enhances a relationship built on strong emotional support. They share a special bond with each other's children. Kim adds LaRosa has always made herself available to provide hands on assistance with her first-born twin daughters who are now adults and have special needs. Kim has three daughters. LaRosa has two sons. Their seventeen year olds were born seven days apart and are very close.

*Note: The "BFF" Award has yet to be established. However, inductive reasoning allows you to objectively conclude that Kim and LaRosa are the primary candidates for this future recognition. In the meanwhile, have a good laugh with a best friend today. You might be the next recipients of the future "BFF" Award.

A best friend pleads the Fifth Amendment

Ask Ms. Anner J. Echols if she is a best friend and she will most definitely plead the Fifth Amendment. Also, knowing about her Miranda Rights certainly helps. However, Ms. A.J. (one of her well known aliases) has a lengthy record.

Ms. A. J. is CEO and founder of AJE Dreamland Productions where "Dreams are made real". This company is located in the heart of the Raleigh Community in Memphis, TN. Ms. Echols works tirelessly, diligently and fiercely to empower the many individuals who come to her. Those who have the opportunity to be tutored and trained by her are guaranteed to develop poise, self-confidence and improved self-esteem.

If a best friend is defined as one who encourages you, supports you and is your confidant, then Ms. Echols adds new meaning to a best friend relationship. She has positioned herself to befriend many in search of that special someone who will allow them to showcase their talents and abilities. She has been that shoulder to cry on, that hand to hold tightly, and that smile that says yes you can. Sometimes, the spoken word is not necessary when more than twenty years of "incriminating" evidence reveals the true essence of a best friend relationship that involves humility and a giving spirit. A.J's love for what she does and love for people sends out a loud message despite her quiet and humble spirit.

Barry and Toy, husband and wife, best friends

His name is Barry Byears, Jr. Hers' is Toy Byears. Besides both having the same last name, what is the connection? They are husband and wife who are also best friends. Toy is 30 years old and is an attractive young woman. She is at the day home provider this morning dropping off Barry Byears, III. When asked if she has a best friend, she responds in a very soft voice, "My husband is my best friend." You look at her and smile. You think this will make an interesting best friend story. You give her your card. She gives you her phone number. You both agree tonight after she gets off work will be a good time to continue this conversation.

Actually, the follow up is the next evening shortly after 7:00 P.M. You and Toy talk by phone and begin with how she and Barry met. They are entering their third year of marriage and they met in high school. They dated for a period and then broke up while still in school. Their paths crossed again after they graduated from Millington High School. Toy states she considers her husband to be her best friend because she can talk and discuss anything with him. She feels totally at ease with him. She states he makes her laugh. They both share a strong love of family, enjoy sports and socializing with friends. They consider Outback Restaurant to be their favorite place to eat. They went there on their first date.

It is apparent as you listen intently to Toy that she enjoys talking about her best friend. She stresses that the two of them have a strong spiritual bond. They were both born in Memphis, TN. They share the same values. She states they can always talk through issues and come to a mutual understanding. Because her husband is her best friend, Toy states they share an even more intimate connection. She states she can honestly say that he is truly her other half and that he completes her in every way.

Obviously, the conversation has to come to an end. More was said than can be written. You contemplate how the best friend relationship is a major factor in our lives. Its significance is quite evident when a young married couple possesses this kindred quality. As Toy would say, "It's a

Best friend discovers new therapeutic venue

Shopping is therapeutic, especially in the case of the female species. Males do run close behind. Nevertheless, as you observed the crowd at of all places the Whole Foods Market on a Saturday morning, you were amazed at the number of shoppers in the store. You could not discern if there were more males than females. Your best friend told you that when it came to health, men could be just as proactive as women.

You are just hanging out with your best friend. You reflect on how for the past ten years she has developed a very strong interest in alternative approaches to maintaining optimum health. You have tried to harbor an open mind, but you continue with the more traditional approach to your health. You love your doctor and everything seems to be going well. You do have a few aches and pains that you contend with, but you assume that it goes with the aging process.

Of course, your health conscious best friend constantly tells you that most people are too accepting of growing old. You have to admit that she has managed to keep her weight under control. She is also not on any medication and her energy level is very high. She works out more than you do. (Actually, you do not work out at all.) You conclude that your love for cooking might be a contributing factor to the different direction that your health is moving.

Your best friend shares all of her latest health discoveries with you. Some you have seriously embraced, but the cost factor can slow you down. On this day, she is encouraging you to try kefir and barley greens. As you observe several handsome men in the store, you think why not.

You honestly enjoy shopping. You are going to give more thought to being independent of your best friend as you add health food stores to your shopping venues. The aging process is causing you to re-examine non-traditional approaches to improving your health. Your best friend said that it really is about being more spiritual minded. You are still trying to grasp that concept. However, for some people eating is therapeutic just as shopping can be. If you can merge the two together in a more enlighten way, then you are ready to board this spiritual plane.

Best friend relationships are enduring

Best friends tend to have an enduring relationship. Sixty years old, Delores Garmon states she and her best friend, Cheryl Jones, have been best friends since grammar school. Delores is now retired but not expired. Still an attractive woman, Delores has a very friendly disposition. As she smiles and talks about her best friend, it's as though she lights up and you also join her in smiling.

Delores shares with you that she and Cheryl usually speak to each other every day. She adds Cheryl keeps an even closer tab on her since she had knee surgery. Cheryl continues to be employed as an OR and Trauma nurse. Delores states their children are grown and gone. She and Cheryl attend the same church. Delores is a musician and Cheryl sings in the choir. Delores states communication has been the mainstay of her best friend relationship with Cheryl. She states they lift each other's spirit. Delores states she also likes Cheryl's personality. They are quite at ease with one another.

You and Delores have met each other in the Tire and Lube Express waiting area at Wal-Mart on Austin Peay Highway in Memphis. It is a Friday afternoon. Delores states she actually lives in Eads, TN near Wolf Chase Galleria. Her best friend lives in Collierville, TN. She states they will be getting together later on to dine out and have a fun evening. She states they especially enjoy O'Charley's and the Macaroni Grill, among other restaurants.

You are definitely enjoying your conversation with Delores. However, you are both anxious to get your Friday evening started. Delores arrived ahead of you. You're both in SUV's. Suddenly, the cashier calls your name. Previously, you had gotten up only to be informed that your name was not called. You were glad Delores was still there to continue conversing with her. You think what a pleasant and interesting woman she turned out to be. You two also manage to laugh over conversations about marriage relationships and appreciating the need to have some independence in your life. As you finally get up to leave, you and Delores exchange goodbyes. You think of the amazing endurance of best friend relationships. You also think that Cheryl is very fortunate to have a wonderful person like Delores for a best friend. No doubt, the feeling is mutual.

Best friends, a senior moment, the bucket list

Sometimes you and your best friend start checking off on your bucket list earlier than you planned. This can happen when one of you has a senior moment. You must always be prepared for this situation.

Perhaps you might get a cancellation call from your best friend thirty minutes before you arrive to go to with her to Davis-Kidd Book Store and then to Olive Garden Restaurant. Before you can ask your best friend why, she hangs ups the phone.

You decide to continue the drive to your best friend's house. She does not seem surprised that you showed up. She is dressed in her bathrobe and shower sandals. You ask if there is something wrong. She shakes her head and sits down on her sofa. You remain standing. You are trying to assess what's going on. Your best friend tells you to sit down by her on the sofa. Suddenly, she reveals without looking at you that she feels life is moving too fast and she wants to check off the first thing on her bucket list before she becomes totally dependent on others.

You remember after seeing the movie, The Bucket List with Morgan Freeman and Jack Nicholson, you both were inspired to compose your own bucket list. That was almost three years ago.

You conclude this is a very serious situation. Your best friend must have something very important to tell you. You try to brace yourself. You will be strong for your best friend.

In a very calm manner, your best friend tells you that it took four attempts for her to put her legs in the correct openings of her underwear when she got out of the shower. All of the openings looked alike to her. Suddenly, she saw herself as helpless. Soon she would become a burden to her family. At that moment, she decided she must do the first thing on her bucket list.

You hold back the urge to laugh. You have experienced a similar situation, but in three attempts. Your best friend is having a senior moment. You ask to look at her bucket list. She points to the coffee table. You pick up the list. Her first item is to go on a trip to Las Vegas for one week. You offer to go with her. You wonder if you can locate your bucket list. You recall meeting Denzel as the first of your twenty things to do.

Best friends build a bridge of love under you and carry you across

A best friend will build a bridge under you and then carry you across. You need not worry about asking for support from a best friend. They connect with you. They feel your joy and your pain. They laugh with you and cry with you.

No matter how much personal tragedy you experience, a best friend is always there to support you, comfort you and hold your hand. A best friend patiently allows you to struggle with the lost of a love one. A best friend knows when to speak and when to keep silent. A best friend is that light at the end of the tunnel. A best friend looks you in the eyes and silently communicates I am here if you need me. A best friend realizes that you need time to process, to digest and to accept that you are going to make it through all the hopelessness, the despair and the pain of heart that is ripping you apart.

You know it will take time to heal from the unexpected loss of a love one. You try to stay focus on the now moment. Somehow with the support of best friends you do not give up all hope. You realize you are not alone. You must hold on and rely on cherished memories of the past to sustain you. A best friend will be your anchor. No matter how far you might sink, a best friend is holding on to the lifeline that will sustain you. They are vigilant, prayerful and encouraging. Nothing can separate the bond of a true friendship. It becomes stronger as you share personal life experiences.

A best friend in Memphis is simply the best. But best friends do travel and so they can be found all over the world. You cherish the vibrations of best friends. They are in harmony with you because they truly love you. They build a bridge of love under you and do whatever it takes to get you across the turbulent waters of grief due to the loss of a dear love one.

Best friends enjoy walking in Memphis

There is a song entitled "Walking in Memphis" by Marc Cohn. Best friends most definitely enjoy walking in Memphis. The song is now the unofficial walking song for best friends. After the song has ended, you will often find yourself repeating, ". . . walking in Memphis. Walking with my feet 10 feet off of Beale."

You will find best friends doing a lot of walking on Beale Street. They will walk from the west end to the east end. Many will repeat this walk several times depending on how many shops and restaurants or clubs they might check out along the way. Morgan Freeman's Ground Zero interrupts a lot of walkers with good intentions. Eel Etc, B.B. Kings, Blues City Café and Hard Rock Café are draws as well and will definitely break your walking momentum.

Best friends who go walking in Memphis have to have other options besides Beale Street. One favorite walking trail is down by the Mississippi River at Ashburn-Coppock Park.

Sometimes best friends can be reluctant about telling you about some of their best walking trails in Memphis. They can be territorial about this. You might have to do some independent research. Some interesting discoveries will include Audubon Park, Lichterman Park, Mud Island, Overton Park, Germanshire Park and Heroes Park. On rainy days, indoor malls are favorite options.

Best friends enjoy walking together because it is an opportunity to bond even closer. As one best friend related, you become more relaxed as you and your best friend walk side by side. You learn more about each other. Conversation topics vary. You enjoy each other's company just doing this simple activity. The companionship motivates you to continue walking on a regular basis.

To sum it up, walking is therapeutic and best friends walking together experience what it really means to be "walking 10 feet off of Beale".

Best friends never die

A best friend never dies. It does not matter that some people might consider that statement apocryphal. Some experiences in life you should not want to undergo to believe in them. Just be prepared when someone tells you that a best friend lives forever in your heart.

Kim Fields of Millington, TN is willing to confirm the truthfulness of the statement that, "A best friend never dies." Kim and her best friend, Alicia, were inseparable until 12 years ago. They became best friends during their teenage years in Hawaii. For the two of them, life was about fun and enjoyment. The beach, the guys and the clubs filled most of their youthful years. Marriage brought Kim to Memphis, TN. Alicia eventually followed. As best friends, hanging out on Beale Street in Memphis became one of their favorite pastimes. Kim loved Alicia's spontaneity. She also described Alicia as very caring. Kim is smiling as she talks about her best friend, but a little sadness surfaces as she interjects that Alicia made some bad choices in life. Kim found herself having to show Alicia some tough love. That was a momentarily painful regression and Kim hastily snaps out of it. She allows the smile again to dominate her facial expression. She adds that Alicia loved to say, "Let's have a cup of cappuccino." You see a sparkle in her eyes. It is apparent that Alicia is still very much a part of her life. You smile too and you find yourself unequivocally convinced that best friends never die.

Special note: This article is dedicated to best friend actress in the TV shows Maude and Golden Girls, Rue McClanahan. Rue made her "transition" on June 3, 2010. Who knows, perhaps she and Alicia have crossed paths and are sipping a cup of cappuccino discussing Kim.

Best friends spotted at Memphis Southern Heritage Classic tailgate party

Best Friends enjoy hanging out at tailgate parties when the Memphis Southern Heritage Classic game is played at the Liberty Bowl. Just ask Marva and Juanetta of Memphis, Tennessee. They were spotted at the tailgate party of Ronnie "Boomer" Williams.

You immediately notice the special chemistry between Marva and Juanetta as soon as they arrive. You observe as they sit together their constant interaction, smiling faces and relaxed attitude. You conclude that they are two ladies who enjoy having a good time and being together. You are drawn to them. You inquire about their best friend status and they both immediately confirmed what you had suspected.

Marva was the more outspoken of the two ladies. Juanetta readily agreed that Marva was the one to answer questions. They have been friends for the past twenty-two years. They still enjoy hanging out together. Marva stated they have a lot in common. She emphasized that they actually think alike. She also shared that they have adopted each other's family. Juanetta's children call her Aunt.

Marva revealed that she was six years older than Juanetta. She stated she sometimes takes on the mother role in their relationship due to the age difference. Nevertheless, there is an obvious mutual respect for each other's opinion that bonds them together. Marva was quick to stress that neither of them "bites their tongue" when it comes to telling each other the truth about a matter. They believe in being "real" with each other.

You admire the genuine love and respect that these two ladies have for each other. Juanetta did manage to add that their twenty-two years of friendship has endured despite periods of separation. Her husband was in the Army and the family traveled in and out of the country. But the separation never impacted the closeness that she and Marva had developed. They were able to stay in touch and continue their close friendship bond.

There is no doubt that these two ladies share an enduring best friend relationship. When you question them about their favorite restaurant in Memphis, they both immediately start grinning. Marva is the one who responds, "Marva's Kitchen of course."

FYI: Congratulations to Jackson State. It's been a long time coming, but a change was bound to come!!!!!!!

Cosmetologist, massage therapist, and all around best friend

In his profession as a licensed cosmetologist and massage therapist, Eugene Tate has often found himself being labeled a best friend by many of his customers. He is the owner and manager of First Touch Spa & Salon in Bartlett, TN. He specializes in hair care, waxing, facials and massages. He often sees his customers every two weeks and a special friendship develops. Some bonds are stronger than others. Eugene finds himself fulfilling the role of a best friend and confidant. He states he has definitely learned to be a good listener.

Sitting in his salon between customers is a rare occasion. However, Eugene was willing to agree to this interview with some apparent curiosity. He has been in the cosmetology business for the past 16 years. He enjoys what he does and has experienced some unexpected rewards. His role as a best friend has allowed him to extend his boundary to customer's family members as well. He recalls with a smile and apparent satisfaction how he befriended and assisted Katisha Burnett, a customer of six years. His role as a best friend and a good listener put him in a unique position. In this instance, he did not just listen and offer advice, but he felt compelled to become actively involved in helping her son, Rodney, to improve his conduct at school. After all, true best friends do not just sympathize. They empathize as well.

Eugene's willingness to intervene as a concerned adult resulted in a 12 years old son no longer wanting to disappoint his mother. Now, an average student is making "A's" and "B's". A love for basketball has been enhanced with participation as a team member. A child maturing and not wanting to bring his mother pain and discomfort has been observed. A child's confidence that perhaps he can be the next Kobe Bryant is an impressive accomplishment.

Eugene's business slogan is "The only touch you'll ever need". The empowering touch of a best friend's help is sometimes all you need. Perhaps you might encounter Eugene as he relaxes at Blues City Café on Beale St. in Memphis, TN. Don't be surprised if the smile on his face is not due to the salad and rib dinner that he is eating, but it is because he's thinking about the changed young man who can seriously dunk a ball.

Ellen Degeneres has a best friend in Memphis

Ellen Degeneres has a best friend in Memphis. This best friend wishes to remain anonymous. That's the uniqueness about being a best friend to the stars. It has a cosmopolitan aspect that those who find themselves in the entertainment business as well as in the news media might have to consider. People in these professions actually have more best friends than the average individual. This is not a mere fan base. These anonymous best friends are devoted and supportive. Ellen's best friend in Memphis is quick to let you know that Ellen is a genuine and caring human being who has style and talent. She is also intelligent, witty, energetic, immutable, sentient, and adds value to the world. They both love music and dancing. Ellen's best friend wants her to continue to shine and smile. Being an optimist, Ellen's best friend is looking forward to giving her a grand tour of Memphis, starting with Elvis' Graceland.

Entertainer, singer, Joe Kent has a best friend

The dynamic singer and entertainer, Joe Kent willingly acknowledges that he has a best friend in Memphis, TN. Also a very outstanding performer of Elvis music, the handsome Mr. Kent points out a mutual love for music bonds him and best friend, Duke Brando, together. Mr. Kent quickly adds that he is especially impressed with his best friend's knowledge of the music industry. They met approximately three years ago. Mr. Brando works closely with George Klein on the Elvis Radio Station on Sirius Satellite Radio, channel 13 in Memphis. He is a noted Elvis Presley historian.

Mr. Kent states he and Duke often hang out at his home after some of his performances. He values his best friend's critiques of his performances. You can check Mr. Kent out at the Rock and Roll Café on Elvis Presley Blvd in Memphis. A friendship of this caliber between an Elvis tribute performer and an Elvis historian has to be quite extraordinary. Despite an age difference of close to 14 years, it can be said that they complement each other as they share their mutual love and respect for the legendary Elvis Presley.

Mr. Kent is a native Memphian. He has been in the entertainment business for over the past 18 years. His love for singing and being jovial as he shares humorous jokes and antics on stage are very captivating. He continues to perform live. He has been on television and appeared in movies. As recently as June 5, 2010, he donated his time to perform at the" FloodFest" 2010 Concert to raise money for Millington, TN flood victims. No doubt, you can appreciate him even more as a musical goodwill ambassador who happens to have a best friend in Memphis.

George and Charlie, best friends 50 years plus

George and Charlie, age 58 and 57 respectively have been best friends for over 50 years. This friendship continues despite the fact that George moved to Indianapolis, Indiana shortly after graduating from Lemoyne-Owen College. Charlie graduated from the University of Memphis and accepted a job offer in Chattanooga. He presently resides in Memphis and is a Major with the Memphis Police Department. George is retired and was in management with General Motors. They both Graduated from Douglass High School in 1970.

George states he feels that their friendship has endured because they shared common interests, similar values and were both focused on career goals early in life. Although they pursued different vocational objectives, they had strong work ethics. Despite living in different states they have maintain contact by phone and whenever George returns to Memphis they manage to find time to be together.

George and Charlie are married and have grown children. George is the father of two beautiful daughters. He also has two grandchildren. Charlie has one lovely daughter and one grandchild.

Charlie stated they have many fond memories of growing up in north Memphis. George's parents and Charlie's mother and stepfather were next-door neighbors. George and Charlie were both members of the Royal Gents social club at Douglass High School. Bowling, playing baseball, playing card games such as spades, and going to the movies filled their leisure time. They even doubled dated together.

George added they had a love for the same type of music. They always enjoyed hanging out with each other. Charlie could not recall any disputes or bad feelings between them.

The close camaraderie that these two men share is very special. You observe a connection that is as strong as two biological brothers. Best friends always seem to be inseparable despite time and distance.

Ground Zero closes, best friends hold the belief it will reopen

The recent announcement of the closing of Morgan Freeman's Ground Zero Blues Club on Sept. 20, 10 was a surprise. However, best friends Gwen and BL believe the doors of this very poplar blues club will open again. They were both there on Saturday night listening to the soulful sounds of Ms. Ruby Wilson. The Legendary Queen of Beale St. exemplified finesse. She song with a soulful and powerful voice that captivated her audience who wanted more and more of those tantalizingly sweet vocal chords.

Gwen and BL made it their business to go to Ground Zero despite Gwen's sprained ankle. They were not disappointed. The food, the atmosphere, the crowd, and the entertainment epitomized what Beale Street is about.

Gwen and BL grew up in South Memphis and graduated from Carver High School. BL was a year ahead of Gwen. Both attended Rhodes College, formerly Southwestern at Memphis. They are currently residents of Raleigh Bartlett Meadows.

The bond between Gwen and BL is based on similar interests, trust and a willingness to offer a listening ear and a helping hand. They are very supportive of each other. They enjoy going to events and social functions together. They also have some mutual friends in common. Both are very active and always on the go. Having a great deal in common due to growing up in the same neighborhood and attending the same college was the catalyst to their friendship being forged into a close bond. They also have mutual respect for each other and they communicate on a regular basis.

Gwen and BL had concluded that Ground Zero was going to be one of their favorite entertainment spots. They were excited about returning again to hear more of the blues according to Ms. Ruby Wilson.

The closing of Ground Zero has to be a huge mistake. Hopefully, the owners/financial backers will see that Ground Zero is essentially one of Beale's Street strongest draws. The place has provided an entertainment venue that cannot be duplicated or replaced. The employees and the manager were committed to providing quality customer service that assured patrons would return time and time again. Who can resist the Ambassador welcoming you with that bellowing voice and enticing smile. No more Ground Zero for Gwen and BL is unthinkable.

Ms. Ruby Wilson, Queen of Beale Street, has a best friend

She is an elegant and talented lady. She has the smooth, satin, and melodious voice that draws you to her and then she simply explodes. You love her sounds and her style. The Queen of Beale Street, Ms. Ruby Wilson, reigns supreme and she reveals to you that she has a best friend.

Being a best friend to the Queen must be very special. Silky Williams of Atlanta, GA is in that unique position. Ms. Ruby discloses they have been best friends for close to 40 years. They stay in touch weekly. She and Ms. Ruby first met at Goldsmith's in Atlanta. Ms. Ruby states she was looking for make-up and Silky escorted her to this area in the store. Ms. Ruby added she did not reveal who she was. She later invited Silky to one of her performances. That was the beginning of a best friend relationship that continues to this day.

Ms. Ruby makes a point of sharing she has lots of best friends. She states they serve different purposes in her life. However, Silky is her "bestest" friend. Ms. Ruby loves Atlanta and tries to visit Silky once a year. They enjoy doing everything together. They are about the same age. They both enjoy Memphis soul food. Silky loves Ms. Ruby's music and has all of her recordings.

Ms. Ruby states she and Silky tell each other everything and do not have to worry about what they share becoming public knowledge. She humorously adds they will always be best friends because they know too much about each other.

After complimenting Ms. Ruby on her exceptional dress style as she shares some photos, you learn two more things about her. She designs the one of a kind outfits that she performs in and she is working on a book entitled "Just Because It's On a Rack, Doesn't Mean It Has To Be Put On Your Back."

The interview at Piccadilly with Ms. Ruby ends. You feel in awe of her presence. You conclude she is a gracious and generous lady. She recently donated her time to sing at a June 5, 2010 Flood Fest concert for Millington, TN flood victims. She is smiling as you get up from the table. You thank her for the interview. She adds, "I've been blessed." She leaves with Evelener Williams, a best friend who serves a different purpose and accompanied her today.

Nat Daddy, my father, my best friend

Imagine you and your best friend being born on historical Beale Street in Memphis, TN. That best friend is Nat Daddy, your father, and the first black deejay in the south. Try to absorb this as you speak at length with Natolyn A. Williams Herron. Her father and best friend, the august Nat D. Williams, entertained WDIA radio listeners over 25 years.

Being raised in Memphis, you were familiar with the famous radio host, Nat D. Williams. You could not recall meeting him in person, but to know Natolyn resonated his presence. She was very captivating as she illuminated many wonderful things about her father and best friend.

Nataloyn states she and her father shared a strong bond. She describes him as intelligent, approachable, and spiritual. A gentle giant of a man, he was also progressive minded and as far as she was concerned ahead of his time. She states he was driven, had an insatiable thirst for knowledge and was a true educator. Every opportunity was seen as a learning experience. He taught her how to swim and type before she could write. The family often drove to historic places in Memphis on Sundays after church.

Nat D. Williams was a strong proponent of human rights and the music industry. As a journalist, he took his family with him to cover the "Little Rock Nine Story". Natolyn interjects that she has met many distinguished political figures and entertainers. B.B. King and Elvis were among them.

Natolyn recalls those special moments when she rode in the car alone with her father. He shared many life lessons with her. She humorously related how he dealt with her militant phase while attending TSU. She said he simply showed up on campus one day. She was informed that an old black man with thick glasses was looking for her. He had come to rescue his daughter. He was the voice of reason. When he spoke, you had to listen. He calmed her young rebellious spirit.

Natolyn is excited about her upcoming 45th class reunion slated for Labor Day weekend. She graduated from Booker T. Washington where her father taught history classes. She informs you that he was a prom sponsor her junior year. She admits she actually danced more with her father than with her date. After all, a best friend and good dancer like Nat Daddy left no room for competition.

No off switch to being a good friend

There is no off switch to being a best friend. Therefore, don't be surprised when your 57 years old best friend calls you up and tells you that she is learning about the modeling business. You have always supported her in all of her past endeavors. You realize this is no exception.

Reflecting back, you recall your best friend is like the forever-moving ever-ready bunny rabbit when it comes to endeavors. Two years ago, she was pursuing sales as her primary interest. She sold everything from legal insurance, cosmetics, identity theft plans, and jewelry.

You recall earlier interest in everything from cake decorating to health supplements. There was the juicing diet fad promotion. There was the interest in Salsa dancing, trampoline jumping and walking on the treadmill every morning. You were supportive. Sometimes you tried to become an actual hand's on advocate.

Your best friend has definitely kept you busy over the years. Sometimes you wonder what would your life have been like without your best friend. You both have always lived in Memphis. You still enjoy the same things, dinning out at Perkins's Restaurant and going to plays at Playhouse on the Square and shopping anywhere and everywhere in Memphis.

Sometimes it appears that having a best friend comes with a great price. But in reality, the special bond that you share is priceless. The dynamics of the relationship can change, but you happily conclude there is no off switch when it comes to being a best friend.

Preserving things of value

From a very early age, we are taught that some things are very valuable in life and must be handled with extreme care. There are the miniature porcelain dishes that belonged to Great Grandma Rose. They can be looked at admiringly, but absolutely no one is to use them or touch them. There is Uncle Shirley's English coin set that can never be traded or sold. Don't forget Cousin Earl's mahogany walking cane that must remain in the corner by the fire place. And it is critical that the 100 years old iron four poster bed in the guest bedroom never be painted, given away or sold outside of the family. These precious items can never be replaced if lost, stolen or destroyed. They are considered part of your connection to your past, your forever-legacy.

Even more valuable is the keeping of a best friend relationship. In fact, a best friend relationship should be guarded and preserved with just as much focus and intensity. It's long-term rewards are often more important than the keeping of family heirlooms. Best friends are vital. They allow a connection to the world in which you live. They are part of the "now" experience and ride along with you as you journey through life. They can come aboard when you are just a toddler or arrive during your middle age. The point being is that you will have a void in your life until you and your best friend's path cross. In fact, the need to preserve things of value becomes more significant when it involves a best friend. This invaluable bonding is often outside of the family network. That is what makes best friends unique and one of the most special things in life. And it is okay to reach out and touch them, hug them and love them forever.

Scientific poll reveals shoes run second to diamonds as a girl's best friend

Do a non-scientific poll of 10 women. Next to diamonds being their best friend, you will discover shoes run a close second. The outfit is the soul of the wardrobe, but shoes are the defining statement. Shoes allow you to "strut your stuff". They are the "wrap up". They take you where you want to go.

The non-scientific results also revealed that these unique best friends add up because you like variety. A woman's closet rarely has only one pair of best friends. The average was thirty. All of the respondents wanted to remain anonymous, especially when one admitted to having 100 plus pairs of best friends.

One individual stated, "Shoes make your day." They can keep you smiling because that is what best friends do. They make you feel good because you know you look good as you promenade through out the day. Best friends support you and shoes definitely do that.

Just as you cannot put a price on friendship, you can't put a price on your shoes. You will cherish them and protect them. You keep track of them. After all, best friends deserve special consideration.

Shoes have favorite hangouts in Memphis. The work place, clubs, and churches ranked the highest. As your best friends, shoes are ready to go everywhere at any time. They know how to be prepared for any occasion. You like them short, tall, medium, or flat. You do not discriminate when it comes to color.

If you are in the market for finding more best friends in Memphis, you have many places to choose from all over town. It is suggested that you start with the malls. Wolf Chase, Oak Court, Mid America Mall, Hickory Hill Mall, Southland Mall and Raleigh Mall are known as best friends hangouts. Of course, it would be acceptable to stop by your favorite jewelry store and check on how some of your favorite diamond best friends are doing. After all, shoes and diamonds reflect your attitude as they grace your style. All participants in the poll agreed that hands and feet make the outfits complete and there is nothing better than a woman with happy feet.

Best friends contemplate living forever

You are enjoying lunch with your best friend at Applebee's Restaurant on Stage Road in Bartlett, TN. You suddenly share with her that you have decided that you want to live forever. Of course your best friend has no verbal response to this comment. She just looks at you with a smile. However, you can tell by her entire facial expression that she is probably thinking how she's gonna win the million dollar lottery today, since you made the commitment to never die.

Of course, it is critical that you offer your best friend a reason for your hanging on to the longevity factor. She probably knows it has to do with your five years old granddaughter. You tell your friend that there is a bucket list that you have made for things to do with your granddaughter. It is important for her to understand that for you growing older means getting better and better because of the things that you have planned for you and your grandchild. You will not focus on aging as meaning getting closer to the exit from this world scene. Instead, you are looking forward to enjoying life with a renewed vigor and determination to be around to also enjoy your great grandchildren and beyond.

Your best friend tells you that she admires you for being so positive. She has never entertained the possibility of this belief in eternity on earth as being an inevitable reality. She did share that she liked the idea. You appreciate your best friend is trying to be open minded. After all, she has grandchildren and she also wants to be around a long time to see them grow and become productive citizens.

One interesting thing you tell your friend is that if eternity was not a likelihood, why doesit comes to mind. You have concluded it is a good thought to want to live forever. It is of course contingent upon good health, wealth and ongoing creativity. To believe in this possibility involves thinking outside the box which requires a quantum leap in the magnificent faith of the human spirit.

When your best friend tells you she should write a bucket list of things to do with her grandchildren, you feel excited. You look forward to comparing your list with hers. You also think her winning that million dollar lottery definitely makes the future look brighter.